Chutneys & Relishes

by Lou Seibert Pappas

Illustrations by
Kathleen Edwards

CHRONICLE BOOKS

SAN FRANCISCO

ACKNOWLEDGMENTS

Thanks to Michel Blanchet, Caroline Engel, Krishna Kopell,
Beth Hensperger, and Virginia Tedrow for sharing their beloved recipes,
and to Cathie Colson for her expertise. Carolyn Miller once again
proved to be an invaluable, delightful editor.

Text Copyright © 1995 by Lou Seibert Pappas
Illustrations Copyright © 1995 by Kathleen Edwards

Design and production: Lory Poulson

Printed in Hong Kong.

Library of Congress Cataloging-in-Publication Data

Pappas, Lou Seibert.
     Chutneys and relishes / by Lou Seibert Pappas :
          illustrations by Kathleen Edwards
     72 p.   165 x 165 cm.
     Includes index.
     ISBN 0-8118-0840-8
     1. Cookery (Relishes)   2. Chutney.   3. Relishes.   I. Title.
TX819.A1P36   1995
641.8'12—dc20   94-43153
                              CIP

Distributed in Canada by Raincoast Books,
8680 Cambie Street, Vancouver, B.C. V6P 6M9

10 9 8 7 6 5 4 3 2 1

Chronicle Books
275 Fifth Street
San Francisco, CA 94103

CONTENTS

Introduction

Just a spoonful of chutney adds a spark to everyday fare, and relishes tantalize the taste buds as they spice innumerable dishes with exuberant flavors.

With their sweet-sour tang and lively heat of chili or ginger, these condiments seem to sharpen the flavors of other foods. Their bold flavors add interest and complexity to simple dishes. Because they contain no fat, these condiments have become even more popular in today's cuisine.

In the West, chutneys are usually cooked and made with fruit, while relishes may be cooked or uncooked and are usually made from vegetables. Our Western chutney originated from the East Indian *chatni*, a condiment of fruit or vegetables cooked with vinegar, sugar, and spices. This is the chutney adapted by the British, the best-known commercial version of which is a mango chutney. But Indian cooking also has an entire category of fresh chutneys, which are usually savory rather than sweet, and usually made of vegetables or herbs. Both types of chutney can range in texture from chunky to smooth and in spiciness from mild to hot.

In an earlier era in America, home preserving provided a way of saving the bounty. Old World emigrés stocked their pantry with glistening jars of apple chutney, corn relish, chili relish, piccalilli, and other condiments, relying on the summer harvest for winter pleasure.

No longer is it a necessity to preserve chutneys and relishes in quantity. Today the ready availability of vegetables and fruits from around the world makes most such foods accessible almost year round. Ideally, of course, preserving should be done at the peak season of local harvest.

Chutneys and relishes are much quicker and easier to prepare in small batches. Many may be stored in the refrigerator for several weeks, eliminating the need for processing in a boiling-water bath. Freezing can soften their texture and thus is not always desirable, although ingredients may be frozen for later preparation.

Part of the fun of preparing chutneys and relishes is customizing them to suit personal tastes. The heat of chili can be turned up or down to suit your preference. The sugar level can be adjusted slightly to please your palate. Brown sugar tends to give a darker color and caramel flavor to condiments. Different vinegars lend their own distinctive nuance.

The preserving equipment needed to make the recipes in this book is minimal. A 4- or 5-quart saucepan with an 8-inch diameter works well. A wooden spoon, a ladle, and a scale come in handy. A food processor and blender can make fast work of chopping, thus shortening the preparation time.

Avoid overcooking chutneys and relishes, as a caramelized taste can result. Cooked condiments will thicken slightly upon standing, and their flavors will improve and mellow with refrigeration.

Containers for storage and serving can range from any hot sterilized glass jars from quilted canning jars to recycled food jars. French confiture glasses with plastic lids are particularly attractive and useful for gift giving. European-style glass-lidded jars with rubber rings and wire closures are available in many sizes. Specialty glasses are available in many attractive shapes.

Most cooked chutneys and relishes keep one to two months or longer in the refrigerator. If you lack the refrigerator or freezer space to store condiments, or wish to make them in quantity for longer-term keeping at room temperature, the U.S. Department of Agriculture recommends hot-water processing all acid fruits and vegetables as a safety measure to avoid food poisoning. All pickled products should be sealed and cooked in a hot-water bath for 10 minutes for room-temperature storage of 8-ounce jars. For larger jars and high altitudes, consult your local county extension service.

To hot-water-process jars, pack chutneys and relishes in hot sterilized jars and seal with lids as the manufacturer directs. Set the jars on a wire rack at least ½ inch high in a stockpot or canner deep enough to allow for 1 to 2 inches of boiling water above the lids and 1 to 2 inches of air space above that. Fill the pan with hot water to cover the lids by 1 to 2 inches, cover the pan, bring to a boil, and boil for 10 minutes. Remove the jars with tongs to a wire rack. Let cool; label and store in a cool, dark place for up to 1 year.

Chutneys and relishes make ideal hostess gifts and look festive in their glass jars. To personalize them, include a label with serving ideas, attaching it with colored yarn, string, or raffia tied with a bow. Two or more condiments packed in a basket are a special treat.

The recipes in this book are easy to achieve. Serving ideas accompany each condiment recipe. A separate recipe section includes dishes that incorporate chutneys and relishes or are especially enhanced by their accompaniment.

With their kaleidoscope of flavors, these condiments will uplift appetizers, salads, sandwiches, curries, grilled foods, and cheeses, and some will even enhance desserts. May you find delight in personalizing your meals with these homemade chutneys and relishes.

Making

Chutneys

and

Relishes

Three-Fruit Chutney

Both fresh and dried fruits flavor this all-seasons chutney. It is exceptional paired with aged Cheddar cheese and whole-grain or walnut bread in the tradition of the English Ploughman's Lunch. In a British pub, the chutney often comes in a little stoneware pot. This chutney also complements grilled sausage, roast duck, venison, beef, pork, or pâté.

1 1/4 cups cider vinegar
3/4 cup packed brown sugar
3/4 teaspoon salt
1 dried red pepper, seeded
2 teaspoons ground ginger
1 teaspoon ground cinnamon
1/8 teaspoon freshly ground black pepper
1/2 teaspoon ground cloves
2 garlic cloves, minced
1 1/4 pounds (about 4) tart apples, peeled, cored, and chopped
1 cup (6 ounces) pitted dried prunes, diced
1 cup (6 ounces) dried apricots, diced

Place all the ingredients in a large saucepan. Bring to a gentle boil and cook uncovered, stirring occasionally, for 40 minutes, or until thickened. Discard the dried pepper. Ladle into hot sterilized jars, seal, and refrigerate. Keeps for 6 to 8 weeks.

MAKES 3 CUPS

Note: Slip the dried pepper into a tea ball during cooking so you can easily remove it.

Granny Smith Apple Chutney

With its spicy citrus tang, this chutney teams superbly with roast chicken, turkey, or pork. Or snuggle it in a cream cheese–slathered bagel or a jack cheese and brown bread sandwich. A Granny Smith tree in my garden supplies bushels of organic fruit for this favorite chutney.

3 pounds (about 9) tart Granny Smith apples, peeled, cored, and diced
2 large onions, chopped
$3/4$ cup packed brown sugar
$1/2$ cup golden raisins
$1 1/4$ cups cider vinegar
Zest of 1 orange, julienned
1 stick cinnamon
$1/2$ teaspoon each salt and ground cloves
$1/2$ cup chopped walnuts, toasted (optional)

Place all the ingredients except the nuts in a large saucepan. Bring to a gentle boil and cook uncovered, stirring occasionally, for about 45 minutes, or until thickened. If desired, stir in the nuts the last few minutes of cooking. Ladle into hot sterilized jars, seal, and refrigerate. Keeps for 6 to 8 weeks.

MAKES ABOUT 5 CUPS

Cranberry-Shallot Chutney

Ideal for the holiday season, this ruby chutney with its intriguing Indian aroma complements roast turkey, pork loin, and duck. West Coast cookbook author and caterer Beth Hensperger adds a spoonful to a slice of pâté or savory cheesecake.

 3 cups (12 ounces) fresh cranberries
 2 large tart apples, peeled, cored, and chopped
 1 1/4 cups packed brown sugar
 1/3 cup raspberry vinegar
 1/2 cup golden raisins
 1/4 cup (1 ounce) finely chopped candied ginger
 1/2 teaspoon each salt and curry powder
 Finely shredded zest of 1 orange
 2 shallots, minced
 3/4 cup (3 ounces) chopped walnuts or pecans, toasted (optional)

Place all the ingredients except the nuts in a large saucepan. Bring to a gentle boil and cook uncovered, stirring occasionally, until thickened, about 20 minutes. If desired, stir in the nuts. Ladle into hot sterilized jars, seal, and refrigerate. Keeps for 6 to 8 weeks.

MAKES ABOUT 4 CUPS

Apricot Chutney

Take advantage of the fleeting apricot season by making this tangy ginger-spiked gem. Mate it with grilled chicken, roast duck, seafood, and meat curries, or serve it with sharp white Cheddar cheese and crackers.

3 pounds firm, slightly green apricots, halved, pitted, and diced (8 cups)
1 large onion, chopped
$1/4$ cup finely chopped candied ginger
$3/4$ cup packed light brown sugar
$1 1/4$ cups cider vinegar
$1/2$ cup golden raisins
2 teaspoons mustard seeds
$3/4$ teaspoon salt
2 cinnamon sticks
1 teaspoon *each* ground cardamom and allspice
$1/2$ teaspoon ground ginger
Tiny piece dried red pepper

Combine all the ingredients in a large saucepan. Bring to a gentle boil and cook uncovered, stirring occasionally, until thickened, about 30 minutes. Ladle into hot sterilized jars, seal, and refrigerate. Keeps for 6 to 8 weeks.

MAKES ABOUT 6 CUPS

Pear-Anise Chutney

The licorice overtones of anise and the heat of ginger and chili punctuate this golden chutney with a lemon tang. Serve it with chicken, turkey burgers, or pork chops, or spoon it onto pork tacos or pita pockets stuffed with feta, cucumbers, and tomatoes. It also completes cream-cheese-and-watercress tea sandwiches. This is the perfect recipe for unripe pears.

 1¼ cups cider vinegar
 1 cup sugar
 3 pounds (about 6 large) firm, slightly green Anjou, Bosc,
  or Winter Nellis pears, peeled, cored, and diced
 1 onion, chopped
 ½ cup chopped red bell pepper
 ½ cup golden raisins
 2 teaspoons finely shredded lemon zest
 ½ teaspoon salt
 2 tablespoons minced fresh ginger or ¼ cup (1 ounce) candied ginger,
  finely chopped
 ¼ teaspoon dried red chili flakes (optional)
 1 teaspoon aniseed

Place all the ingredients in a large saucepot. Bring to a gentle boil and cook uncovered, stirring occasionally, for 40 minutes or until thickened. Ladle into hot sterilized jars, seal, and refrigerate. Keeps for 6 to 8 weeks.

MAKES ABOUT 5 CUPS

Gingered Purple Plum Chutney

This sensuous plum sauce perks up roast chicken, leg of lamb, grilled sausages, and curries. My friend Virginia Tedrow makes it for a charming hostess gift for friends. Since the prune plum season is brief, she often buys extras and stashes them in the freezer for a batch come spring.

2 pounds Italian prune plums, halved, seeded, and quartered (5 cups)
1 cup packed brown sugar
1 cup cider vinegar
1/8 teaspoon dried red pepper flakes
1 teaspoon salt
1 teaspoon each ground mustard and mustard seeds
1 garlic clove, sliced
1 large sweet onion, chopped
1/2 cup (2 ounces) finely chopped candied ginger
1 cup golden raisins

Place all the ingredients in a large saucepan. Bring to a gentle boil and cook uncovered, stirring occasionally, for 25 to 30 minutes or until thickened. Ladle into hot sterilized jars, seal, and refrigerate. Keeps for 6 to 8 weeks.

MAKES 4 CUPS

Gingered Cherry Tomato Chutney

Partner this burnt orange–hued condiment with smoked turkey or chicken, or add it to a feta cheese and brown bread sandwich for a tantalizing sweet and salty interplay. If you are lucky enough to grow your own Sweet 100 cherry tomatoes, this is a perfect use for them.

    1 pound (2 1/2 cups) cherry tomatoes
    1 cup sugar
    1 lemon, thinly sliced and quartered (including the peel)
    1 cinnamon stick, broken into pieces
    1/3 cup distilled white vinegar
    1/2 teaspoon salt
    4 whole cloves
    1/4 cup (1 ounce) finely chopped candied ginger

Place all the ingredients in a large saucepan. Bring to a boil, reduce heat, cover, and simmer for 10 minutes. Uncover and boil gently, stirring occasionally, for 35 to 40 minutes, or until syrupy and thickened. Ladle into hot sterilized jars, seal, and refrigerate. Keeps for 6 to 8 weeks.

MAKES 1 1/2 CUPS

Mango Chutney

This spicy-hot chutney augments many dishes: chicken and melon salads, shrimp and lamb curries, pork roast, grilled spareribs, and cold meats. It falls into the pleasantly tart, rather than ultra-sweet, category.

$^2/_3$ cup cider vinegar
$^3/_4$ cup packed light brown sugar
$1^1/_2$ pounds firm mangoes, peeled, seeded, and cubed (about 3 cups)
$^1/_2$ cup chopped onion
1 chopped peeled tart apple
$^1/_2$ lime, peeled, very thinly sliced, and chopped
2 tablespoons minced fresh ginger, or $^1/_4$ cup (1 ounce) candied ginger, finely chopped
$^3/_4$ teaspoon ground cinnamon
$^1/_4$ teaspoon each ground allspice and cloves
$^1/_4$ teaspoon dried red pepper flakes or small piece dried red pepper
$^1/_2$ teaspoon salt
2 garlic cloves, minced
$^1/_3$ cup dark or golden raisins

Place the vinegar and sugar in a heavy saucepan and bring to a boil. Add all the remaining ingredients, bring to a boil, turn off heat, and let stand for 30 minutes. (This will plump the fruit and allow it to absorb flavors and sugar.) Boil gently, uncovered, stirring occasionally, until the chutney has thickened, about 45 minutes. Ladle into hot sterilized jars, seal, and refrigerate. Keeps for 6 to 8 weeks.

MAKES ABOUT 3 $^1/_2$ CUPS

Blueberry-Port Chutney

This piquant wine-laced chutney glorifies game, duck, lamb, or pork. It also makes a delicious topping on French toast, pancakes, waffles, frozen vanilla yogurt, or toasted-almond ice cream. If you are lucky enough to locate huckleberries, they are a superb substitute.

Finely shredded zest from 1 orange
1 cinnamon stick, broken into pieces
$\frac{1}{2}$ teaspoon each whole allspice and whole cloves
$\frac{1}{2}$ cup red wine vinegar
$\frac{1}{2}$ cup sugar
2 tablespoons ruby port
2 cups (12 ounces) fresh or frozen blueberries

Tie the orange zest and spices in cheesecloth or place in a tea ball; place in a medium saucepan with the vinegar and sugar. Bring to a boil, lower heat, and simmer for 5 minutes. Add the port and the berries and boil gently, uncovered, for 5 minutes. With a slotted spoon, remove the berries to a hot sterilized jar. Raise heat and boil gently until juices are slightly thickened, about 10 minutes; pour over the berries. Seal and refrigerate. Keeps for 6 to 8 weeks.

MAKES ABOUT 1 $\frac{1}{4}$ CUPS

Green Tomato Relish

Once the frost hits, surplus green tomatoes will find a flavorsome use in this sprightly relish. Pair it with meat and cheese sandwiches, hamburgers, or cold cuts. Spoon it on a tuna sandwich or grilled fish steaks. Or serve it on an appetizer tray to spoon over Cheddar, Swiss, or Brie cheese–topped crackers.

1½ pounds (about 4) green tomatoes, cut into 1½-inch dice
1 large onion, cut into 1½-inch dice
1 pound (about 3) tart green apples, peeled, cored, and diced
⅓ cup golden raisins
1 cup sugar
1¼ cups cider vinegar
½ teaspoon each salt and ground ginger
1 tablespoon mustard seed
2 garlic cloves, minced
1 green or red jalapeño chili, seeded and chopped, or ¼ teaspoon
    dried red pepper flakes (optional)

Finely chop the tomatoes and onion in a food processor or by hand. Place all the ingredients in a large, heavy saucepan, bring to a gentle boil, and cook uncovered, stirring occasionally, for 30 minutes, or until thickened. Ladle into hot sterilized jars, seal, and refrigerate. Keeps for 6 to 8 weeks.

MAKES 4 CUPS

Onion-Cassis Relish

This elegant black currant and onion relish is sensational with chicken, duck, lamb, and beef. It is a specialty of Michel Blanchet, the consulting chef on the Crystal cruise lines, who uses it to dollop poached chicken-breast pinwheels.

    1 pound (about 3) onions, finely chopped
    3/4 cup red wine vinegar
    1 cup dry white wine
    1 cup black currant syrup (*sirop de cassis*)
    1/4 cup sugar
    1 teaspoon salt

Combine all the ingredients in a large saucepan, bring to a boil, cover, lower heat and simmer 15 minutes. Uncover and cook at gentle boil, stirring occasionally, until all the liquid is evaporated, about 1 1/2 hours longer. Ladle into hot sterilized jars, seal, and refrigerate. Keeps for 6 to 8 weeks.

MAKES ABOUT 1 1/2 CUPS

Note: Look for black currant syrup in a gourmet shop or liquor store.

Piccalilli

Hamburgers, barbecued meats, and grilled fish get a boost from this minced vegetable pickle that probably stems from colonial times in India. It makes good use of those end-of-the-season green tomatoes hanging forlornly on the vines.

4 green tomatoes, cut into 1-inch chunks (2 cups)
6 ounces cabbage, cut into 1-inch chunks (2 cups)
1 small red bell pepper, cored, seeded,
   and cut into 1-inch chunks
1 large onion, cut into 1-inch chunks
2 teaspoons each celery seed and mustard seed
1 1/2 teaspoons salt
1/2 teaspoon ground allspice
1 cup cider vinegar
2/3 cup sugar

Process the tomatoes, cabbage, bell pepper, and onions in a blender or food processor until finely minced. Turn into a large saucepan and add the remaining ingredients. Bring to a gentle boil and cook uncovered for about 25 minutes, or until thickened. Ladle into hot sterilized jars, seal, and refrigerate. Keeps for 6 to 8 weeks.

MAKES ABOUT 3 CUPS

Chili Relish

Choose this lively tomato-based relish to enhance meat loaf, hamburgers, omelets, grilled fish, and tacos. Its gentle chili heat enlivens black beans, burritos, and lentil soup as well. Adding the spices the last half hour of cooking allows them to retain more flavor. For a variation with a hotter, richer overtone, add a dried smoked chipotle chili during cooking.

4 pounds (about 12) tomatoes
1/2 cup packed brown sugar
2 onions, chopped (1 1/2 cups)
2 green bell peppers, cored, seeded, and chopped
3 garlic cloves, minced
1 tablespoon salt
1 1/2 cups cider vinegar
2 teaspoons ground cinnamon
1 teaspoon each ground allspice and ground ginger
1/2 teaspoon ground cloves
1 small dried red pepper, seeds removed
1 dried smoked chipotle chili, soaked in boiling water
    and chopped (optional)
2 tablespoons minced fresh basil

Slip the tomatoes into a pan of boiling water for 30 seconds to loosen their skins; lift out and run under cold water, then peel. Chop in a food processor or by hand. Place all the ingredients except the spices and basil in a large saucepan, bring to a gentle boil, and cook uncovered, stirring occasionally, for 2 hours; add the spices and cook 30 minutes longer, or until thickened. Add the basil the last few minutes of cooking. Ladle into hot sterilized jars, seal, and refrigerate. Keeps for 6 to 8 weeks.

MAKES 4 CUPS

Garden Relish

Zucchini, carrots, onions, and peppers make a colorful relish for hamburgers, Mexican casseroles, grilled meats, and fish. Or tuck a couple of spoonfuls into a Jarlsberg cheese and brown bread sandwich.

1 pound (3 large) zucchini
2 large carrots, peeled
1 yellow onion
1 small red bell pepper, cored and seeded
1 1/2 teaspoons salt
1/2 cup distilled white vinegar
3 tablespoons sugar
1 teaspoon each celery seed and dill seed
1/2 teaspoon dry mustard
1/3 cup pitted oil-cured black olives, Manzanilla cocktail olives, or ripe olives

Shred the zucchini in a food processor or with a grater. Fold in a towel and let stand a few minutes, then squeeze to remove the moisture. Shred the carrots, onion, and pepper, and place all the vegetables in a large saucepan with all the remaining ingredients except the olives. Bring to a gentle boil and cook uncovered, stirring occasionally, for 10 minutes, or until crisp-tender. Stir in the olives. Ladle into hot sterilized jars, seal, and refrigerate. Best when used within 1 week.

MAKES ABOUT 5 CUPS

Mediterranean Fennel and Olive Relish

Licorice-flavored fennel, tangy orange zest, and assertive black olives create a zestful condiment to mate with grilled fish steaks, scallops, prawns, pork, lamb, or even pasta. This relish also makes an attractive first-course salad mounded on a bed of radicchio and arugula, and encircled with orange segments.

> 1/2 cup fresh orange juice
> 2 tablespoons finely shredded orange zest
> 2 tablespoons balsamic vinegar
> 1 fennel bulb (about 1 pound), chopped (3 cups)
> 1 small red onion, chopped
> 2 tablespoons chopped feathery fennel leaves
> 1/4 cup pitted oil-cured black olives
> Salt and freshly ground black pepper to taste

In a medium bowl, combine the orange juice, orange zest, and vinegar. Stir in the remaining ingredients. Cover and chill. Best when used the same day.

MAKES 4 CUPS

Cilantro-Corn Relish

Sweet white corn kernels are the base for a superb chili-spiked relish. Adjust the chili heat up or down to suit your fancy or add a splash of liquid hot pepper seasoning. This colorful Southwestern-style condiment augments enchiladas, burritos, turkey burgers, and grilled meats.

4 ears white or yellow corn, or one 10-ounce package
    frozen corn kernels
1 teaspoon ground cumin
1 small red onion, chopped
$1/2$ cup cider vinegar
$1/4$ cup sugar
2 teaspoons fresh oregano, or $1/2$ teaspoon dried oregano
1 small jalapeño chili, seeded and chopped,
    or dash of liquid hot pepper seasoning
$1/2$ teaspoon salt
1 red bell pepper, cored, seeded, and diced
$1/3$ cup minced fresh cilantro

Cut the kernels from the ears of corn; you should have about 2 cups. Toast the cumin in a medium saucepan for 1 to 2 minutes, or until aromatic. Add the onion, vinegar, sugar, oregano, chili, and salt, and bring to a boil. Simmer for 5 minutes. Add the bell pepper and corn and simmer for 3 to 4 minutes, or until the corn kernels are cooked through. Spoon into a container, cover, and refrigerate. Stir in the cilantro just before serving. This is best when used within 1 week.

MAKES ABOUT 2 CUPS

Eggplant-Shiitake Relish

This eggplant spread makes a versatile appetizer or a first course: Ring it with red and gold plum tomatoes or stuffed grape leaves; spoon it into mushroom caps; or mound it onto a plate lined with romaine leaves as scoops. Or serve it with lavosh or sesame crackers, accompanied with a bowl of oil-cured black olives. It's also good with grilled lamb or white fish.

1 large eggplant (about 1¼ pounds)
2 shallots, minced
4 ounces stemmed shiitake or unstemmed
   button mushrooms, chopped
1 tablespoon olive oil
2 tablespoons fresh lemon juice
3 garlic cloves, minced
1 tablespoon minced fresh basil
3 tablespoons minced fresh flat-leaf (Italian) parsley
⅓ cup plain yogurt
Salt and freshly ground black pepper to taste
¼ cup sunflower seeds, toasted, or pomegranate seeds for garnish

Preheat the oven to 400°F. Place the whole eggplant in a baking pan and bake uncovered for 30 to 40 minutes, or until soft. Dip the eggplant into cold water. Prick with a fork and squeeze out the juices, then peel and let cool. In a small skillet, sauté the shallots and mushrooms in oil until soft, about 3 minutes. In a blender or food processor, puree the eggplant with the mushrooms and shallots, lemon juice, garlic, basil, and parsley. Stir in the yogurt and season with the salt and pepper. Turn into a container, cover, and chill. Sprinkle with sunflower seeds or pomegranate seeds to serve. Best when used within 2 or 3 days.

MAKES 2 CUPS

Cilantro-Mint Chutney

With its brilliant green color and sweet-hot flavor, this condiment sparks curries and grilled fish. Or use it as a dip for shelled cold prawns or pappadums. Depending on the heat of the chili, be either lavish or discreet when serving it.

1 1/4 cups lightly packed fresh cilantro leaves (1 bunch)
1/3 cup lightly packed fresh mint leaves
Juice of 2 limes
Salt to taste
1 green jalapeño chili, seeded and minced

Process the cilantro, mint, lime juice, and salt in a blender or food processor until finely minced. Add the chili to taste and blend in. Best when used the same day.

MAKES 1 CUP

Red Pepper Relish

This scarlet relish mates ideally with roast turkey or duck. Tuck it in a lamb and feta pita pocket or a Jarlsberg and ham whole-grain sandwich.

 1³/4 pounds (about 6) red bell peppers, cored and seeded
 1 lemon, thinly sliced and quartered (including the peel)
 1 cup sugar
 ³/4 cup distilled white vinegar
 ¹/2 teaspoon salt
 1 tablespoon mustard seed
 1 teaspoon coriander seed

Coarsely chop the peppers in a food processor or by hand. Place in a large saucepan with all the ingredients. Bring to a boil, reduce heat to a gentle boil, and cook uncovered, stirring occasionally, for 1 hour, or until syrupy and thickened. Ladle into hot sterilized jars, seal, and refrigerate. Keeps for 6 to 8 weeks.

MAKES 1¹/2 CUPS

Fiery Ginger-Tomato Relish

This fresh-tomato relish packs a flavor punch and is a versatile condiment for many foods: bean soups, Mexican dishes, grilled fish, barbecued pork or lamb, pasta, and risotto.

1 pound (about 4) Roma tomatoes, peeled and coarsely diced
3 green onions, cut into 1/4-inch-thick diagonal slices
1 serrano or jalapeño chili, seeded and thinly sliced,
    or 1 small dried red pepper, split
2 tablespoons olive oil
1/2 teaspoon cracked black pepper
1 teaspoon yellow or black mustard seeds
2 tablespoons minced fresh ginger
2 garlic cloves, minced
1/2 teaspoon ground turmeric
1 teaspoon ground cumin
3 tablespoons packed brown sugar
1/2 teaspoon salt
1/3 cup rice vinegar

Stir together the tomatoes, onions, and chili in a large bowl; set aside. Heat the oil in a small skillet and sauté the black pepper, mustard seeds, ginger, garlic, turmeric, and cumin for 1 to 2 minutes; stir into the tomato mixture. Add the brown sugar, salt, and vinegar to the pan and heat until the sugar is dissolved. Pour over the tomato mixture. Cover and refrigerate for 2 days before using. This is best when used within 4 to 5 days.

MAKES 2 1/2 CUPS

Cucumber-Yogurt Relish

A favorite in Greece—where it goes by the name of *tzatsiki*—this refreshing accompaniment complements kabobs, roast lamb, prawns, grilled salmon, and halibut. Or serve it as a first course with cherry tomatoes, oil-cured olives, and sesame crackers or country bread.

2 cups plain yogurt
1 English cucumber, or 2 large regular cucumbers
Salt to taste
1 tablespoon fresh lemon juice
2 tablespoons olive oil
3 garlic cloves, minced
1/4 cup minced fresh flat-leaf (Italian) parsley
    or fresh mint leaves
Freshly ground black pepper to taste

Place the yogurt in a sieve lined with a double thickness of cheesecloth and let drain over a bowl for 2 hours to thicken slightly; discard the whey or use for another purpose. Halve the cucumber(s) lengthwise (peel if using regular cucumbers), then thinly slice. Place in a colander, sprinkle lightly with salt, and let drain for 1 hour. Squeeze the cucumber slices gently between paper towels to remove more moisture. Combine the yogurt, lemon juice, oil, garlic, parsley or mint, and cucumber slices in a bowl. Season with pepper, cover, and chill. Best when used the same day.

MAKES ABOUT 3 CUPS

Yogurt-Pear Chutney

This cool, fruity condiment lends an intriguing spiciness to curries and other Indian fare and offers a refreshing contrast to chili-spiked dishes. Choose a rich, naturally thick yogurt in preference to a nonfat yogurt.

    3/4 teaspoon cumin seeds
    1 cup plain yogurt
    1/2 teaspoon minced fresh ginger
    1 teaspoon grated lemon zest
    1 Bartlett, Anjou, or Comice pear, peeled and chopped
    2 tablespoons chopped fresh mint leaves (optional)

Heat the cumin seeds in a small dry skillet over medium heat just until lightly toasted, about 40 seconds. Turn into a bowl and stir in the yogurt, ginger, lemon zest, pear, and mint, if desired. Best when used the same day.

MAKES 1 3/4 CUPS

Tomato–Red Onion Chutney

A wonderful all-purpose relish, this goes together in a jiffy. With its intriguing overtones of five-spices and basil, it offers an appealing alternative to a chili-spiked condiment. Spoon a colorful mound alongside grilled fish, chicken, or sausage, or serve it as a cool accompaniment to pasta.

3 tablespoons red wine vinegar
1 teaspoon packed brown sugar
4 Roma tomatoes, diced (about 1 pound)
1 small red onion, minced
1/4 cup minced fresh basil
1/8 teaspoon ground Chinese five-spices
Salt and freshly ground black pepper to taste

Mix all of the ingredients together in a bowl. Best when used the same day.

MAKES 1 1/4 CUPS

Note: If desired, add 1 minced green jalapeño chili, or to taste.

Indian Carrot Chutney

The tang of orange and curry powder flavors this savory chutney. Serve it with pita bread triangles, sesame crackers, or corn chips.

1 small onion, chopped
4 carrots, peeled and sliced
$1/2$ cup water
$1/3$ cup orange juice
Zest of 1 whole orange, finely julienned
Salt and freshly ground black pepper to taste
1 teaspoon curry powder, or to taste
$1/4$ cup plain yogurt
1 tablespoon coarse-ground mustard
1 tablespoon fresh lime juice
Fresh green or purple basil or arugula leaves for garnish

Place the onion, carrots, and water in a medium saucepan. Cover and simmer for 10 minutes. Add the orange juice, orange zest, salt, pepper, and curry powder, and simmer for 10 to 15 minutes longer, or until the vegetables are tender and the juices are evaporated. Turn into a blender or a food processor, add the yogurt, mustard, and lime juice, and puree until smooth. Turn into a bowl, cover, and chill for several hours. Garnish with basil or arugula leaves. Best when used within 2 or 3 days.

MAKES 2 CUPS

Using

Chutneys

and

Relishes

Appetizers

Sandwiches

Entrees

Two Dozen Quick Chutney Appetizers

Brioche with Chicken and Chutney

Top brioche or egg bread slices with sliced smoked chicken or turkey breast and top with Apricot Chutney, Tomato–Red Onion Chutney, or Three-Fruit Chutney and an arugula sprig.

Duck and Plum Canapes

Toast baguette slices and top with sliced roast duck, a spoonful of Gingered Purple Plum Chutney, and a sage or basil leaf.

Tortilla Nibbles

Sprinkle tortilla chips with shredded Monterey jack or Muenster cheese and bake in a 350°F oven until melted; top with Chili Relish or Green Tomato Relish.

Smoked Turkey Canapes

Toast baguette slices, spread with garlic-butter, and top with smoked turkey and a dab of Onion-Cassis Relish or Gingered Cherry Tomato Chutney and a sprig of arugula.

Bread Sticks and Cheesy-Relish Dip

Dip garlic-flavored bread sticks in a chive cheese dip topped with a layer of Chili Relish or Green Tomato Relish.

Apricot Chutney and Brie

Place a wedge of Brie on an ovenproof plate, spread with Apricot Chutney and slivered blanched almonds, and bake in a preheated 350°F oven for 8 minutes, or until warm and soft. Serve with toasted baguette slices or crackers.

Red Pepper Relish and Cream Cheese

Spread Red Pepper Relish or Green Tomato Relish on a mound of natural cream cheese and serve with sesame crackers or peppered water biscuits.

Pita with Eggplant-Shiitake Relish

Cut whole-wheat pita bread into triangles and fill with Eggplant-Shiitake Relish and a sprig of arugula.

Pork and Gingered Cherry Tomato Chutney

Spread squares of toasted crusty bread with Dijon mustard and top with roast pork and Gingered Cherry Tomato Chutney or Red Pepper Relish and a sprig of arugula.

Cucumber, Feta, and Chili Relish

Top cucumber slices with feta cheese and a dollop of Chili Relish.

Mushrooms Stuffed with Carrot Chutney

Spoon Indian Carrot Chutney in mushroom caps and top with chopped fresh chives or a fresh basil sprig. Or serve the relish with blue corn or lime-chili tortilla chips, or jícama sticks and sesame crackers.

Tiny Stuffed Potatoes with Goat Cheese and Relish

Make a hollow in cooked small red new potatoes, fill with fresh mild white goat cheese, and top with Chili Relish or Red Pepper Relish. Or brush 1/4-inch-thick slices of baking potatoes with olive oil, roast in a preheated 425°F oven for 15 minutes or until cooked through and crispy, and top with cheese and chutney.

Tortellini and Chili Relish

Serve hot cheese or spinach tortellini with a bowl of Chili Relish as a dip.

Havarti and Relish

Top pita crisps with sliced Havarti and a spoonful of Red Pepper Relish.

Pears and Chutney

Top wedges of Comice, Anjou, or Bartlett pears with sliced Fontina cheese or Maytag or Oregon Blue cheese, a dab of Gingered Cherry Tomato Chutney, and a few toasted pine nuts.

Bagel Wafers with Cheese and Lox

Spread toasted bagel wafers with cream cheese, Onion-Cassis Relish, and lox or smoked trout.

Chicken and Chutney Appetizers

Cut cooked chicken or turkey breast into bite-sized pieces, wrap each morsel in a spinach leaf, and skewer with a toothpick. Dip in a mixture of $1/4$ cup *each* sour cream and lowfat mayonnaise, 1 teaspoon curry powder, 2 tablespoons Mango Chutney, and 1 teaspoon grated orange zest.

Apple, Jack, and Chutney

Cover slices of Granny Smith apples with sliced dry Monterey jack or Kasseri cheese and a spoonful of Three-Fruit Chutney.

Ham Roll-Ups with Chutney Cheese

Spread Black Forest ham or other sliced ham with natural cream cheese and Mango Chutney, roll up, and skewer with a toothpick.

Apricots Stuffed with Cheese and Chutney

Fill apricot halves with Explorateur or Saint-André cheese and dollop with Mango Chutney or Gingered Purple Plum Chutney.

Crostini with Asiago and Red Pepper Relish

Butter and toast baguette slices or country bread, and top with sliced Asiago and Red Pepper Relish.

Plums Stuffed with Mascarpone and Chutney

Fill plum halves with mascarpone and Gingered Purple Plum Chutney or Apricot Chutney. Shower with toasted slivered almonds.

Sun-Dried Tomato Bread with Lamb and Relish

Top slices of sun-dried tomato bread or olive bread with roast lamb and Onion-Cassis Relish and garnish with fresh mint or basil sprigs.

Walnut Bread and Gorgonzola Canapes

Toast walnut bread, cut into fingers, and top with Gorgonzola and Pear-Anise Chutney or Granny Smith Apple Chutney.

Figs and Pears with Prosciutto and Chutney Dip

Figs and pears draped with prosciutto make a luscious appetizer when cloaked with a chutney-spiked sauce. Try two kinds of melon, such as honeydew and Crenshaw, in place of the figs and pears on another occasion.

3 ounces very thinly sliced prosciutto, cut into 1-inch-wide strips
6 fresh black figs, stemmed and halved
2 Anjou, Comice, or red Bartlett pears, halved, cored, and sliced

Chutney Dip
1/3 cup *each* sour cream and plain yogurt
2 tablespoons *each* fresh lime juice and thawed orange juice concentrate
2 tablespoons Mango Chutney or Apricot Chutney

Wrap a strip of prosciutto around each piece of fruit. To prepare the chutney dip: Combine all the ingredients in a blender or food processor and blend until almost smooth. Turn into a serving bowl. Place on a platter and surround with the prepared fruits. Offer wooden toothpicks for guests to skewer the fruit and dip into the sauce.

MAKES ABOUT 2 DOZEN APPETIZERS

Blue Corn Tortillas, Brie, and Chutney

Top warm Brie with a favorite chutney for a fast, zesty dip for blue corn chips.

One 4-ounce wedge of Brie or Teleme cheese
About 1/2 cup Red Pepper Relish, Pear-Anise Chutney,
    or Fiery Ginger-Tomato Relish
Blue corn tortilla chips

Preheat the oven to 350°F. Place the cheese on an ovenproof serving dish and bake just until soft and heated through, about 8 to 10 minutes. Top with relish or chutney. Surround with chips for dipping into the cheese and relish.

MAKES ABOUT 2 DOZEN APPETIZERS

Shrimp and Cheese Nachos

This almost-instant appetizer multiplies with ease to accommodate almost any number of guests.

> 2 cups blue or yellow corn tortilla chips
> 1 cup (4 ounces) shredded Monterey jack cheese
> 1/3 cup Chili Relish or other favorite hot chutney or relish
> 6 ounces cooked small bay shrimp or fresh or
>   thawed frozen crab meat
> 2 green onions, chopped

Preheat the oven to 350°F. Spread the tortilla chips on an ovenproof plate and sprinkle with the cheese. Spoon on the chutney or relish. Sprinkle the shrimp or crab and green onions over all. Bake for 10 to 15 minutes, or until the cheese melts.

MAKES 4 TO 6 APPETIZER SERVINGS

A Dozen Chutney and Relish Sandwiches

Smoked Turkey and Red Pepper Relish Sandwich

Spread seven-grain bread lightly with Red Pepper Relish and fill with sliced smoked turkey or chicken, sliced white Cheddar or Monterey jack cheese, and a few sprigs of arugula or basil.

Ham, Emmentaler, and Granny Smith Apple Chutney on Toast

Spread whole-grain toast lightly with Dijon mustard and fill with thinly sliced ham, sliced Emmentaler cheese, Granny Smith Apple Chutney, and leaf lettuce.

Pastrami, Jarlsberg, and Gingered Plum Chutney on Rye

Spread rye bread lightly with Dijon mustard and Gingered Purple Plum Chutney and layer with sliced pastrami, sliced Jarlsberg cheese, and red leaf lettuce.

Grilled Sausage and Three-Fruit Chutney on Country Bread

Spread crusty country bread with Three-Fruit Chutney and layer with thinly sliced grilled Italian sausage, sliced Fontina cheese, and spinach.

Roast Lamb, Feta, and Cranberry-Shallot Chutney in Pita Bread

Cut a pita bread in half and fill with cold sliced grilled or roast lamb, crumbled feta cheese, Cranberry-Shallot Chutney, alfalfa sprouts, and a few sprigs of arugula or basil.

Almond Butter and Three-Fruit Chutney Toasts

Spread toasted whole-grain bread with almond or peanut butter and cover with Three-Fruit Chutney or Gingered Cherry Tomato Chutney.

Egg Salad and Garden Relish Sandwich

Lightly butter Russian rye bread and fill with egg salad, Garden Relish or Tomato–Red Onion Chutney, and leaf lettuce.

Ploughman's Lunch

Present Granny Smith Apple Chutney, Three-Fruit Chutney, or Apricot Chutney in a small ramekin alongside whole-wheat bread and sliced aged Cheddar cheese.

Chutney and Cheese Quesadillas

Heat an 8-inch flour tortilla in a skillet, sprinkle with shredded Monterey jack or Cheddar cheese, spoon over a ribbon of chutney—Gingered Plum, Granny Smith Apple, or Apricot—and when the cheese melts, fold and serve at once.

Smoked Trout and Gingered Cherry Tomato Chutney on French Bread

Spread crusty French bread lightly with mayonnaise and top with smoked trout, Gingered Cherry Tomato Chutney, and leaf lettuce.

Shrimp, Avocado, and Mango Muffins

Lightly butter and toast split English muffins, cover with sliced tomatoes, cooked small bay shrimp, sliced avocado, and a spoonful of Mango Chutney or Red Pepper Relish.

Goat Cheese, Watercress, and Mango Chutney Tea Sandwiches

Spread thinly sliced good-quality white bread with fresh mild white goat cheese or natural cream cheese, Mango Chutney or Apricot Chutney, and watercress sprigs. Cut into triangles.

Turkey Fajitas

Flour tortillas filled with grilled turkey or pork get a flamboyant lift with Chili Relish or Garden Relish. Or for a refined partner, try the Onion-Cassis Relish.

8 ounces boneless turkey breast or pork tenderloin, sliced 1/2 inch thick
1 tablespoon olive oil
2 garlic cloves, minced
1 shallot, chopped
1/4 cup dry white wine
1 tablespoon Dijon mustard
Four 6-inch flour tortillas
Chili Relish, Garden Relish, or
    Onion-Cassis Relish

Place the meat in a nonaluminum dish. In a small bowl, mix together the oil, garlic, shallot, wine, and mustard. Coat the meat with the mixture and marinate at room temperature for 1 hour. Grill over medium-hot coals, turning once, until cooked to desired doneness, about 10 to 12 minutes. Or, place in a preheated broiler 3 inches from the heat and cook for about 10 minutes. Meanwhile, wrap tortillas in aluminum foil and warm in a preheated 350°F oven or on the grill for about 10 minutes. Slice the meat thinly on the diagonal, divide it among the hot tortillas, and spoon a ribbon of relish over each. Roll up and serve at once.

MAKES 2 SERVINGS

East West Salmon

Ginger, lemongrass, and garlic imbue fish fillets with an expressive flavor.

    2 teaspoons soy sauce
    1 teaspoon packed brown sugar or honey
    1 teaspoon minced fresh ginger
    1 teaspoon minced fresh lemongrass or grated lemon zest
    1 garlic cloves, minced
    Two 5-ounce salmon, orange roughy, mahi-mahi,
        or shark steaks or fillets
    Green Tomato Chutney, Tomato–Red Onion Chutney, or Mango
        Chutney for garnish

Place the soy, brown sugar, ginger, lemongrass, and garlic in a nonaluminum dish; add the fish steaks or fillets and turn to coat. Let sit at room temperature for 30 minutes. Broil in a preheated broiler 3 inches from the heat, or grill over medium-hot coals, turning once, for 3 to 4 minutes per side, or until desired doneness. Serve with a spoonful of chutney on top of each fish steak or fillet.

MAKES 2 SERVINGS

Pork Satés

In Amsterdam, Indonesian rijstaffel (rice table) restaurants feature spicy satés, or meat kabobs, along with an impressive succession of two dozen or more other dishes. Turkey breast works well in this easy, make-ahead entree.

> 2 teaspoons minced fresh ginger
> 1/4 cup Mango Chutney
> 2 tablespoons fresh lemon juice
> 1 tablespoon soy sauce
> 1 garlic clove, chopped
> Dash liquid hot pepper seasoning (optional)
> 1 pound boneless pork loin or turkey breast,
>   cut into 1-inch pieces
> 1/3 cup roasted cashews or peanuts, minced

Puree the ginger, chutney, lemon juice, soy sauce, garlic, and optional pepper seasoning in a blender until smooth. Thread the meat on skewers, place in a shallow nonaluminum dish, and coat with the marinade. Let sit at room temperature for 1 hour. Broil 3 inches from heat in a preheated broiler or over medium-hot coals for about 8 to 10 minutes, or until cooked through, turning to brown all sides. Roll in nuts to coat lightly, and serve.

MAKES 4 SERVINGS

Seafood Curry Bombay

Offer a choice of chutneys and relishes to show off this shrimp and crab meat curry for a party entree. To obtain a vibrant curry flavor, seek out an ethnic or gourmet market for a Madras curry powder.

3 tablespoons butter
4 shallots, minced
2 garlic cloves, minced
3 tablespoons flour
2 tablespoons Madras curry powder
$1/2$ teaspoon ground ginger
2 teaspoons grated lemon zest
1 cup homemade or canned low-salt chicken broth
    or bottled clam juice
1 cup half-and-half
$1/4$ cup dry sherry
8 ounces each cooked small bay shrimp and
    fresh or thawed frozen crab meat
Salt and white pepper to taste
Hot steamed rice for serving
Mango Chutney and Green Tomato Chutney for serving
Chopped green onions, toasted coconut, and toasted
    slivered almonds for serving

In a large saucepan, melt the butter and sauté the shallots and garlic until translucent, about 3 minutes. Sprinkle with flour, curry powder, ginger, and lemon zest; stir and cook for 3 minutes. Gradually add the broth or clam juice and half-and-half, stirring until thickened. Stir in the sherry and seafood and heat through. Season with salt and pepper. Serve over rice, with a choice of chutneys and garnishes arranged in small bowls.

MAKES 4 SERVINGS

Curried Chicken Salad in Papaya Boats

Papaya halves make intriguing edible salad bowls for chicken salad. Another time use small cantaloupe halves or pineapple rings or spears for the fruit base.

Curry-Chutney Dressing
1 teaspoon curry powder
1/3 cup sour cream or lowfat mayonnaise
1/3 cup plain yogurt
3 tablespoons Mango Chutney
2 tablespoons fresh lime juice
Zest of 1 lime

2 cups (1 pound) diced cooked chicken or turkey
1/2 cup sliced celery or diced jícama
1 cup seedless red or green grapes
2 small papayas, halved and seeded
Leaf lettuce or butter lettuce leaves
1/4 cup chopped macadamia nuts or pistachios

To make the dressing: In a small skillet, heat the curry powder for a few minutes until aromatic. In a blender or food processor, blend the sour cream or mayonnaise, yogurt, chutney, lime juice and zest, and curry powder. In a large bowl, mix the chicken or turkey, celery or jícama, and grapes with the dressing. Arrange the papayas on salad greens on individual plates. Spoon a mound of chicken salad into each papaya bowl. Sprinkle with the nuts.

MAKES 4 SERVINGS

Roast Chicken Indienne

Mango chutney gives this Indian-style chicken a flavorful glaze. Serve this dish, with its pretty fruit garnish, as a colorful main course for company.

> 1 broiler-fryer, quartered, or 4 chicken leg-and-thigh quarters
>   (about 3 pounds)
> Salt and freshly ground black pepper to taste
> 1 cup fresh orange juice
> 1/3 cup Mango Chutney
> 1/2 teaspoon ground cinnamon
> 1 teaspoon Madras curry powder
> 1/2 cup homemade or canned low-salt chicken broth
> 1/3 cup golden raisins
> 1/4 cup sliced almonds
> Cantaloupe spears or papaya slices and red or
>   green seedless grape clusters for garnish

Preheat the oven to 425°F. Arrange the chicken skin-side up in a greased baking dish; sprinkle with salt and pepper. Bake for 10 minutes. Meanwhile, combine the orange juice, chutney, cinnamon, curry powder, broth, and raisins in a small saucepan and simmer uncovered until slightly thickened, about 10 minutes. Pour the sauce over the chicken, reduce the oven temperature to 350°F, and continue baking, basting frequently, for 35 to 40 minutes longer, or until the chicken is tender. Sprinkle with the nuts the last few minutes of baking. Serve with a garnish of melon or papaya and grapes.

MAKES 4 SERVINGS

Hot Sausages and Grapes

Glazed hot grapes and chutney lend an instant flair to specialty sausages. You can count on this dish for a last-minute supper with charm.

    2 bratwurst, mild Italian sausages, or fresh chicken-apple
        or herbed pork sausages (about 10 ounces)
    1 teaspoon unsalted butter
    4 ounces seedless green or red grapes
    ¼ cup dry white wine
    Granny Smith Apple Chutney, Three-Fruit Chutney,
        or Cranberry-Shallot Chutney

Place the sausages in a small saucepan and barely cover with water. Bring to a boil and simmer very gently for 10 to 15 minutes, or until cooked through; drain. Add the butter to the pan and sauté the sausages, turning to brown all sides. Add the grapes and cook until heated through. Add the wine and boil until the juices are reduced by half. Spoon the sausages and grapes onto hot plates and accompany with chutney.

MAKES 2 SERVINGS

Note: Instead of the grapes, sauté 4 ounces sliced mushrooms or 1 red bell pepper halved, cored, seeded, and cut into strips, along with the sausage.

Grilled Lamb and Vegetable Kabobs

Thread the vegetables and herb-scented lamb on separate skewers to control the cooking time of each.

Marinade
1/3 cup dry white wine
2 tablespoons olive oil
2 tablespoons fresh lemon juice
2 garlic cloves, minced
2 teaspoons minced fresh rosemary or oregano,
    or 1/2 teaspoon dried rosemary or oregano
Salt and freshly ground black pepper to taste

1 1/2 pounds boneless lamb, cut into 1 1/2-inch cubes
2 Japanese eggplants, cut into 1/2-inch-thick slices
1 *each* red and green bell pepper, halved, cored, seeded
    and cut into 1 1/4-inch pieces
2 zucchini, cut into 1/2-inch-thick slices
Onion-Cassis Relish or Tomato–Red Onion Chutney for serving

To make the marinade: Combine all the marinade ingredients in a small bowl. Thread the meat and alternate the vegetables on 4 skewers. Place the skewered meat and vegetables in a shallow nonaluminum dish, and pour the marinade over, turning to coat. Marinate at room temperature for 1 hour. Grill over medium-hot coals or broil 3 inches from heat in a preheated broiler, turning to cook all sides, for 10 to 15 minutes, or until the meat is medium rare and the vegetables are crisp-tender. Accompany with relish or chutney.

MAKES 4 SERVINGS

Note: As an alternative, 4 boneless lamb steaks cut from the leg can substitute for the boneless lamb cubes. Grill the steaks, without skewering them, for about 10 to 15 minutes.

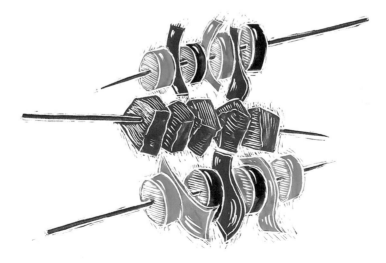

Guadalajara Picadillo

Picadillo, which literally means "minced meat," is a traditional Mexican filling for tacos and enchiladas. In this version it turns into a succulent company stew. Offer melon and papaya crescents with a squeeze of lime for dessert.

1 pound boneless pork shoulder, cut into 3/4-inch pieces
1 tablespoon olive oil
1 small onion, finely chopped
2 garlic cloves, minced
1/4 cup Chili Relish
1/2 cup tomato sauce
1 tablespoon *each* red wine vinegar and packed brown sugar
1/4 teaspoon ground cinnamon
Salt and freshly ground black pepper to taste
1/4 cup homemade or canned low-salt chicken broth
3 tablespoons *each* dried currants and minced fresh cilantro
Hot flour tortillas, guacamole, and Cilantro-Corn Relish or
    Tomato–Red Onion Chutney for serving

In a large saucepan, sauté the meat in oil until browned on all sides. Add the onion and cook until soft. Add the garlic, Chili Relish, tomato sauce, vinegar, brown sugar, cinnamon, salt, pepper, broth, and currants. Cover and simmer for 40 minutes, or until the meat is tender, stirring occasionally. If desired, make in advance and reheat. Sprinkle with cilantro at serving time. Accompany with hot flour tortillas, and guacamole and Cilantro-Corn Relish or Tomato–Red Onion Chutney for topping the picadillo.

MAKES 4 SERVINGS

Lentil and Lamb Stew

For an appealing winter supper, accompany this homey casserole with crusty country bread and a fennel, pear, and red pepper salad. The stew will mellow in flavor when made a day in advance.

1 cup lentils
3 cups water
1 pound lean ground lamb or beef, preferably coarsely ground
1 tablespoon olive oil
2 large onions, finely chopped
1 teaspoon ground cumin
3 garlic cloves, minced
4 carrots, peeled and shredded
2 teaspoons minced fresh oregano, or 1/2 teaspoon dried oregano
1/3 cup Chili Relish
2 cups homemade or canned low-salt chicken broth
1 cup dry red wine
Salt and freshly ground black pepper to taste
Sour cream or yogurt for serving
Three-Fruit Chutney, Granny Smith Apple Chutney,
    Pear-Anise Chutney, or Tomato–Red Onion Chutney for serving

In a medium saucepan, cook the lentils in water for 20 minutes, or until barely tender. In a large, heavy saucepan, sauté the meat in the oil until browned. Add the onions and cumin and sauté until transparent, about 5 minutes. Add the garlic, carrots, oregano, chili relish, and broth; bring to a boil, cover, and simmer for 10 minutes. Add the lentils, wine, salt, and pepper, and simmer 10 minutes longer, or until the lentils are tender. Serve in bowls with a dollop of sour cream or yogurt and chutney.

MAKES 4 SERVINGS

Index

Table of Equivalents

The exact equivalents in the following tables have been rounded for convenience.

US/UK
oz=ounce
lb=pound
in=inch
ft=foot
tbl=tablespoon
fl oz=fluid ounce
qt=quart

Metric
g=gram
kg=kilogram
mm=millimeter
cm=centimeter
ml=milliliter
l=liter

Oven Temperatures

Fahrenheit	Celsius	Gas
250	120	1/2
275	140	1
300	150	2
325	160	3
350	180	4
375	190	5
400	200	6
425	220	7
450	230	8
475	240	9
500	260	10

Liquids

US	Metric	UK
2 tbl	30 ml	1 fl oz
1/4 cup	60 ml	2 fl oz
1/3 cup	80 ml	3 fl oz
1/2 cup	125 ml	4 fl oz
2/3 cup	160 ml	5 fl oz
3/4 cup	180 ml	6 fl oz
1 cup	250 ml	8 fl oz
1 1/2 cups	375 ml	12 fl oz
2 cups	500 ml	16 fl oz
4 cups/1 qt	1 l	32 fl oz

Length Measures

1/8 in	3 mm
1/4 in	6 mm
1/2 in	12 mm
1 in	2.5 cm
2 in	5 cm
3 in	7.5 cm
4 in	10 cm
5 in	13 cm
6 in	15 cm
7 in	18 cm
8 in	20 cm
9 in	23 cm
10 in	25 cm
11 in	28 cm
12 in/1 ft	30 cm

Weights

US/UK	Metric
1 oz	30 g
2 oz	60 g
3 oz	90 g
4 oz (1/4 lb)	125 g
5 oz (1/3 lb)	155 g
6 oz	185 g
7 oz	220 g
8 oz (1/2 lb)	250 g
10 oz	315 g
12 oz (3/4 lb)	375 g
14 oz	440 g
16 oz (1 lb)	500 g
1 1/2 lb	750 g
2 lb	1 kg
3 lb	1.5 kg